Beachcomber

Also by Colleen Keating and published by Ginninderra Press
A Call To Listen (Shortlisted, Society of Women Writers
NSW Book Awards 2016)
Fire on Water (Highly Commended, Society of Women Writers
NSW Book Awards 2018; Nautilus Award – Silver 2017)
Hildegard of Bingen: A poetic journey (Winner, Poetry,
and Winner, Non-fiction, Society of Women Writers NSW
Book Awards 2020; Nautilus Award, Silver, 2019)
Desert Patterns (Highly Commended, Poetry, Society of
Women Writers NSW Book Awards 2020)
Olive Muriel Pink: Her radical & idealistic life – A poetic journey
Soft Gaze, with Michael Keating (Picaro Poets)
Brush of Birds (Picaro Poets)
Landscapes of the Heart, with John Egan (Picaro Poets)
Shared Footprints, with Michael Keating (Picaro Poets)
Mood Indigo, with Pip Griffin (Picaro Poets)
Mists of Time, with Decima Wraxall (Pocket Poets)

Colleen Keating

Beachcomber

Acknowledgements

Many of these poems have appeared in journals and anthologies. I am grateful to the editors of poetry journals for their encouragement and dedication to poetry, especially to the editors of Ginninderra Press.

For their critique, affirmation and support, whether face to face, email or Zoom, I would like to thank Norm Neill and fellow poets of the Wednesday Evening Poetry Group at NSW Writing Centre, Rozelle; Pip Griffin and the Fellowship of Australia Writers (City); the Women Writers Network. Thanks to Ron Wilkins and our U3A Poetry Appreciation group (Epping) for their friendship.

My special thanks to Pip Griffin for her sustained encouragement, including via email and phone during the lockdown of 2021, and for her close edit and proofreading of the collection.

My loving appreciation to Michael for his constant presence and inspiration.

To our grandchildren, Lachlan, Thomas, Tyler, Jacinta,
Cameron, Edison, Dominic, Eleanor, Gemma,
Darcy and Ethan.
May they always have the beachcomber curiosity.

Beachcomber
ISBN 978 1 76109 242 8
Copyright © text Colleen Keating 2022
Cover image: Dmitry Demidov from Pexels

First published 2022 by
GINNINDERRA PRESS
PO Box 3461 Port Adelaide 5015
www.ginninderrapress.com.au

Contents

Foreword	11
Beachcomber	
almost dawn	15
evocation	16
light play	17
beachcomber	19
whimsy	21
after the storm	23
bombora	24
low tide	25
lying on the beach	27
lake theatre	28
a morning song	31
my rosetta stone	33
veranda people	35
Pacific	36
anamnesis	37
Beautiful World	
a beautiful world	41
a serious thing	43
privileged moment	45
haiku	46
grandma's recipe book	47
knotted	49
time	50
chocolate box	51
bells	52
after the spring rain	53

A Song for the Tree

a song for the tree	57
haiku	59
the nest	60
world of wings	61
lamentation	63
in waiting for the jacaranda	65
morning glory	66
old pepper tree	67
resilience	68
a frisson of gold at the centre	69

Never Can We Mourn

a new mea culpa	73
palisade	75
The Gully	76
never can we mourn	77
resignation syndrome	79
rock-a-bye baby	81
we are sorry	82
Christchurch	83
after the massacre	84
all the birds	85
war is over (if you want it)	86
at the controls	87
naked before the gods	88
law of hubris	89
mudras	90
a landscape called humanity	91

Enigma

delphic visitor	95
regret	96

leitmotiv	97
ritual	98
winter	99
enigma	100
memory	101
for my father	102
horizon	103
pondering ducks	104
wind	105
our country bypassed	106

Black Summer

armageddon	111
boxing day, 2019	113
code red	115
inferno	117
bearing witness	118
cry for a river	119

When you can only take photos from the window

autumn equinox	123
pandemic	124
sea of uncertainty	126
note to self	127
when you can only take photos from the window	128
thanks	130
in lockdown	132
the fiddlewood tree in autumn 2020	134
womb-mother	135
the ocean in my heart	136
reciprocity	138

Walking quiet ways
  in search of the superb fairy wren   141
  walking quiet ways   144
  dawn walk   146

A Glad Tomorrow
  garden of the gods   151
  face time by the moon   154
  little mother   155
  sore knees   156
  L Plates   158
  the world through children's eyes   160

Notes   162

Most gulls don't bother to learn more than the simple facts of flight –
how to get from shore to food and back.
For most gulls, it is not flying that matters, but eating.
For this gull though, it was not eating that mattered, but flying.
More than anything else Jonathan Livingston Seagull loved to fly.
– Richard Bach

Foreword

Moon shell, who named you? Some intuitive woman I like to think.

I shall give you another name – Island shell. I cannot live forever on my island. But I can take you back to my desk. You will sit there and fasten your single eye upon me. You will make me think, with your smooth circles winding inward to the tiny core, of the island I lived on for a few weeks. You will say to me 'solitude'. You will remind me that I must try to be alone for a part of each year, even a week or a few days and for part of each day, even for an hour or a few minutes in order to keep my core, my centre, my island quality.

You will remind me that unless I keep the island quality intact somewhere within me, I will have little to give others or the world at large. You will remind me that a woman must be still as the axis of a wheel in the midst of her activities; that she must be pioneer in achieving this stillness, not only for her own salvation, but for the salvation of family life, of society, perhaps even of our civilisation.

from *Gift of the Sea* by Anne Morrow Lindbergh

Beachcomber

In difficult times always carry
something beautiful in your mind.
– Blaise Pascal

almost dawn

he turns
arms cocoon me
in an aura of warmth
his breath tingles
in the dip of my neck

my hand plays
reaches the wells of his desire
i hear him sigh

his hand moves over me
with the confidence of a cellist

vibrating
we lie together
curled
in the almost dawn

evocation

drink the sea
devour rocks
sharp and briny
swallow the light
that stirs and satiates

scoop up the ocean
let it wash through you
furrow and ripple
every wrinkle and scar
the treasure is within

the expanse is you
the expanse is me
we are not held by the sea
we are the sea
in its tangle
with Neptune's necklace
honour avowed

no longer a need
to cork sea air in a bottle
to inhale   to hold
in the dusty cramped city

we are the wisdom
of this wildness
our oneness claimed
untamed
boundless and free

light play

these are the rocks where at dawn some see visions
near here with the waves and spray   or they say they see visions

the rocks glisten and no one else is here at this time
somewhere around here is where they see visions

these are the only outcrops of rocks though that keep changing
with the tides from which some always say they see visions

light illumines from an ancient sight out of the shadows
sometimes foaming sometimes flashing a glitter of visions

what can be seen in mirrored or reflecting shine
frightens many and tells others not to fear visions

beach walkers passing these rocks sometimes find gifts
from the spindrift of sea in a glimmer of visions

and gaze out to the rocks where waves crash and retreat
carving the curves that play the light in a dazzle of visions

there's a tale of an island with outcrops of rocks coral and seaweed
already old   before dim light of our time and soft gleam of visions

where selkies sun on the rocks called Ron Mor Skerry
play with waves and spray in a spangle of visions

for an evil king Balor   with fear of a prophesy
that a grandson would one day be ruler   had murderous visions

imprisoned his daughter with twelve serving women
in a remote seaside cave away from all visions

disguised as a woman   a man came to their aid   giving each a child –
Balor seeing these births that confounded the visions

like Herod sent soldiers to kill all the babes   hurled them to sea
where they came to be ancestors of seals in our visions

now maybe these seals with faces of humans play by the rocks
are seen by those not dim of eye   at dawn in golden light visions

beachcomber

came looking for i don't know what*

i savour the cool balm
of your watery expanse
stretching awake   your heart
ebbing and flowing
reminds me to keep going

stayed   kept looking

my hand traces
around memories
stones
un-spun
knowing there is still more

left and kept looking

i catch the colours
of your eye
       in blue air
add them to my treasure chest
hidden under the bed

stayed and never stopped looking

the pinkest of pink clouds
        drift on the wet sand
        a hermit crab crawls
                from a coconut husk
                a sea hawk hovers
                        over the dunes

looking for i don't know what

i gather
with golden sand of gladness
tiny bubbles of froth at the edge of the waves
a light burden for the journey

of never finding i don't know what

* inspired by the twentieth-century mystic Thomas Merton

whimsy

yesterday an unflinching southerly
whipped a frenzy
pounded at the sand bank
wreaked havoc along the coast
riled up a cavernous sea monster
devouring all in its wake
stirred the bombora from slumber
its rocks like bones bared
pointed and sharp
a fury exposed
it foamed and frothed
no one's friend

today liquid-silver waves
spool and unspool
along the sand
a mellow silken mantle
deepens to emerald green
over a sleeping bombora
its gifted treasure
scattered for the beachcomber
and lover of wet sand underfoot
in a whimsy
it wings and whirls
a welcome friend

a passer-by would never know
the treachery it conceals below
only intimate companions
those who walk and talk
with it in all its moods

after the storm

on the rocky ledge she stands
confronts the crashing waves

that roar in like tigers
to devour her

she reads the weather
like one reads maps

whip of wind
wildly plays in her hair

sting of salt on her fresh red cheeks
a smile on her face

bombora

now out there it rears its steely back
the rocks and coral stack like stoic statues
splatter the sea that rips and roars like a rutting

stag   now it's Proteus rising from the sea
can you hear that old Triton blow his wreathèd horn
warning us all to pray our beaded prayers

it lies forlorn   when the winds are still
and the half moon rises on a back-
lit sky   in this crucible of dying

and being born   now there's hardly a stir
this deep blue sheet needs an angel's hand
from the pool of Bethsaida for its tidal surge

its mask of jewels and cloak of Saturn ripples
show no mercy for those who cling for life

low tide

Poseidon has decreed
the sea hears his ancient name
the quiet waters of the lake
harken to the moon's whisper
obey the seductive summons
bustle busily along
down the well worn path
to their ancestral ocean home

in their wash and wake
waves like an eraser
work to leave a clean slate

sand and rocks   bare and free
delight in the sun's warmth
taste briny breeze
on their naked skin
children run
with buckets   spades   nets
to venture and explore

where once was deep
crabs scuttle into crevices
of exposed rock for hide and seek
fingerling school in shallow shoals
tease amongst reeds and sea grass
a boat tilts on a sand bank   marooned
and fisherfolk fish from shore
to wait out this tidal interlude

pelicans cormorants egrets
come to feed and bask
seagulls come to scavenge
their arrowed footprints and red beaks
stencil the wet sand

i come wandering
ponder the metamorphosis of the beach
enchanted with golden sand eddies
i wade out to a pool
amongst exposed rock
remember childhood adventure stories
caves pirates and treasure islands
of being overawed by this god
who rules the sea

lying on the beach

in leafy-pandanus shade
a floppy summer hat
covers my face

and through its plaited fibres
sky shimmers   purple-blue   red and gold

ocean unaware of its charm
stretches languidly towards me
with a lullaby
my breath eavesdrops on its rhythm
warm sand pillows me
and sifts between my toes

i stay all morning
one with sand and sea and sky
being all this
it being all me

lake theatre

morning throws back its curtain
its stage a ragged island
man-made with dirt from the quarry

the water from the mine ribbons
a deep dark lake
refuge to long-legged
spoonbills   blue herons and egrets

over the the crown of a hill
light swings in
creates a moody scene
cinematic action
panning into tall tongues
of reeds on the apron of the lake
a family of egrets rummage
the sun spotlights
their luminous white plumage

all is hushed
but for the ding of bellbirds

centre stage   a charm of swallows
too fast to count   turn
bank   wheel   then swoop   snap up
flying insects with their wide fringed bills
and dip low over water   Narcissus in a mirror

a solitary spoonbill dredges the mud
in dialogue with two ibises
and at our feet fairy wrens skitter
with footlight chatter

in the eddy
three purple swamp-hens
forage in the reeds
their iridescent blue
holds our attention

from the wings out of the scrub
a fox stalks   orange furry tail
taut in anticipation
it slinks   silent soft pads
snoops with its black-tipped nose
in the grass
its eyes stare silently at the hens

we stand as audience
unable to breathe
we stand   part of the performance
statue still   struck by the insolent show
in awe at the subtle purity of this creature
it steals closer
creeping closer
creeping
with crack of a twig
and alert fast eyes
comes the denouement

cacophony of sound
air full of feather and wing
blue   white   tips of red
long legs stretched upward
reflected ribbon-like in the lake

the fox swiftly turns   stops
stares at us   disappears
the island like a stoic solid friend
embraces all
quietness descends

a morning song

the morning dims with its complexity of dreams
i watch you standing near the bed
in my hiking coat
the sleeves too short and it far too small
and you saying *I hope you have plenty of poetry*
in your pockets for me to read while I'm gone.
then i see the last of the light catch your back

it could be once i enjoyed space
the space between the organ-pipe closeness
of tree trunks
the space where the light gets in

i crave for your return
to breathe you
to be in your orbit   both earths to the sun

i don't have to be in the same room
i don't have to be near you
as long as your movements
are disturbing my aura
i know if you leave on an errand
the silent stillness is unbearable

when i don't get up early in the mornings
like you
i love to watch you watch me
all curled up and sleepy still in bed
and hear you murmur
how lucky you are
i want to answer
if you only could fathom
'how lucky i am to have you'

i love it in the day with others
the secrecy in our look   our nods
the way we hold ourselves
and know the feeling in each other

sometimes i stay up and write
while you read in bed
but when i hop in next to you
i love your little shuffle into me
and how you sigh
when i put my hand
onto your heartbeating chest
to journey dream worlds together

my rosetta stone

'whatever else is going on in life, look for beauty' – anon

pondering sad news
the waves lap
purr at my ankles
writing their daily lines
beige scrawls   tuffed serifs in sand

yesterday you growled like a wild cat
spat out crashing waves
as words of shock and loss
hurled debris at my feet
nothing contained   nothing controlled

a small grey rock
emerges on the ebb   falls at my feet
its inner colour shines –
even in this early grizzled light

i receive it   a gift from the sea
hold it in the palm of my hand
smooth and silent
imagine its story
buffeted battered and broken
tossed tumbled and turned

its presence now is its voice

i step back and stand staring out
from horizon to horizon
        suffering stretches forever
the sea holds answers like embedded secrets

my words fumble like staccato notes
my questions fall into silence

waves lap gently at my ankles
continue their scribble on the sand
i hold my gift
an ancient rosetta stone
to decipher this pain

veranda people

sea-loving dwellers
cling to the edge

scan out to the deep
live in its daze

fenced by break of waves
fish-catching   net-trawling
sand-tramping   dream-playing
castle-building   kite-flying
wave-breaking   surf-riding
boating   sailing and whale-watching

hypnotic horizon holds their gaze
on the edge   looking out

Pacific

how you catch me unaware
trip my heart with sheer delight

how you freely dance without a care
lift my soul in radiance of light

how you sing in all your moods
embrace my presence forever bright

how you erase all fear and panic
with a freshness to excite

ah how your indwelling haunts me
a never-changing   ever-changing sight.

anamnesis

i reach down to gather shells
my age-spotted hand slips
between the waves
small pink fingers of the child in me
lift shells   ocean glass

startled and curious
it is through her eyes i marvel
catch fleeting beams of light
golden pearl   sienna   emerald green

the child runs with playful waves
curling in and around her toes
surfs a 'yes' on their swell
held by core beat of the sea

she builds a sandcastle decorated
with shell and stone and seaweed
digs a moat
and walls
        and walls
        against the creep of tide
        under bruised afternoon sky

Beautiful World

A child said, What is the grass? fetching it to me with full hands;
How could I answer the child? I do not know what it is any
more than she.
– Walt Whitman

a beautiful world

at the party i sit back
watch the action from the side

frivolity centres the room
spills out onto the deck

my daughters laugh
in the kitchen
sampling each others specialities
the men outside   beer in hand
enjoy the sizzle of the barbecue

i watch their little ones
busy at make-believe
they are growing fast
each in their own way

the eldest   now eight years old
is worried about the dolphins
what if they choke on the plastic and all die

the four-year-old responds
i can hear the dolphins in grandma's big shell

i remember my whispered words
as i held each for the first time
welcome little one
it is a beautiful world

now the world waits for them
silent   boisterous   open

their shining eyes also wait
and nested in hope
my heart aches

a serious thing

a brazen sky   already
precocious   bright before its time

leaves riffle
in the tops of trees
half-heartedly
to conserve their energy

birds fuss
their housekeeping done early

my mind curls up
cocoons into a prickly echidna ball
behind closed blinds
remembers childhood summers
their stinging ring   brittle incendiary smell
dart of grasshoppers   dry brown grass
fire-breathing air   respite
when my father   home from work
piles us into his car
to picnic by the coolness of the Peel

now for this heart in hiding
there will never be enough
of seasonal highs and lows
i may wilt like a flower plucked
on this overheating day
but tingle at the miracle to be alive

face time my daughters umbrellaed by the pool
with mercury at forty degrees celsius
another daughter
half a world away   her mercury minus two

just to be alive
on this drip-dry strip-off day
or a rugged-up steely cold day
could this be what Mary Oliver means
when she writes
it is a serious thing   just to be alive

privileged moment

in the window   a diamond crystal hangs
throws a throng of colour
indigo   red   azure blue

my daughter   within whom new life stirs
sleeps on the lounge
her book *The Kite Runner* fallen open

my mother's presence –
her grandma's light
appears in slants
transparent   golden
arms angel-like outstretched

in this room   spirit of ages
circles in spheres of love
as light on the wall quivers

i sit writing at the table
stillness of the space between
broken only by exhausted breathing
waiting.

haiku

magnolia bud
my daughter
waits to give birth

grandma's recipe book

'A precious mouldering pleasure –'tis –
To meet an antique book' – Emily Dickinson

you clutch it from the trunk
hold it high
in veneration   as you would a parchment
of polished vellum
lapis lazuli and gold leaf illumined

then fumble pages   stained
dog-eared   exercise books
stitched together
faded red wool

her recipes poems of instruction
filled days with joy
flutter of pages   magpie song

you feel her whitened hands
guide your small ones to knead the dough
hands floured   even noses tickled
with floured laughter
and the smell of her banana bread

wingless scraps of yellowed newspaper
Woman's Day cuttings   trimmed   glued
hand written recipes   margin hints
steeped in aromas of pot roast
need a white-gloved archivist's touch

bygone tastes of the heart
brush your tongue,
jams   jelly   conserves
from her summer garden

her first Christmas fruit cake without him
pages turn heavy   some bleed with tears
ration lists   war bonds
all fits into you as a manuscript
fits into antiquity

a kitchen table mystic my Grandma
she scribed in pen and ink
all the colours of resilience

knotted

forty years ago
you asked at a local macramé class
who are you
the question still blooms for both of us

in a recent walk around your garden
dried pods of aster and zinnia
bristled
we plucked handfuls
dropped them in the bag
among the haiku books
you were returning

back home
before i had time to plant them
bursting seeds from the bag
escaped and spread
on oat-coloured wings
like friendship memories
embedding wherever they fell
on my jumper   near my bed   desk
on the carpet
even in the car

i gathered   planted   nurtured them
yet stragglers still appeared at odd times
caught in odd places   the way
our friendship has been knotted
in all the fragrances of our lives
planted and still growing
blooming into the new

time

a boundless field
in the middle of the day
sunny and endless
a sanctum of certainty
circles   green and golden

even the slow toll of shadow
arms   with shade
the forever

like drops of sand
time eases in
unfurls with melt of Salvador clocks
each momentary shudder
a keen glint
in a runaway world

when a white knuckled hand
reaches out to hold it back
it's as slithery
as a silver mackerel

chocolate box

a holiday overseas
to see the relatives

children skittish
chocolate box of options
an array of smells and colours
potpourri of sights and sounds

adventures   escapades –
change of guard at Buckingham Palace
guillotine at London Tower
cruising the Thames   Wax Museum
cathedrals   castles   churches
the London Eye
mushy peas and Devonshire teas

Channel Tunnel into Paris
sweet as brûlée and melting cream
Arc de Triomphe   the River Seine
vistas from the Eiffel Tower

galleries   gardens   Disney World
Moulin Rouge
soufflé   escargots and baguettes

closing the lid on the month
after donuts at Waterloo Station
i turn to the kids
well what was your favourite?

without hesitation
playing with our cousins
and the barbie at Aunt B's

bells

they are the sound of stones tinkling in a brook high in the hills
a lamb's urgent cry for its lost mother   jingle
of coins in a child's pocket at the door to a lolly shop

and if you can imagine the hum of a bee
your ear to the tree touches its hairpin sound
if you can hear the toll of marching feet fade

and hear a mother lay war medals on a cedar dresser
and the rain on corrugated tin in the depth of a gun-metal sky
then you know too the clang of a door slammed in your face

and the silence that reverberates   you could know
the peal of children laughing in a school yard
or the clatter of a grandchild's cereal-laden plate on the tiles

as he in his high chair claps with delight
you might even know the raindrops spilling from leaf to leaf
in the old elm tree   and the butcher-birds' warble in the eucalypt

igniting the dawn   perhaps you hear grains of sand sifting
through the narrow neck in the soft light of a dying day
and the knell of rocks in a river on its slow flow to the sea

after the spring rain

from my window grass and leaves
glisten with joy
or are they tears of sorrow

so far it is a fickle spring
the coats and scarves stored away
at the weekend for next winter
are out again

yet the rain is welcome
after a long dusty dry
the air is fresh and clean
and i take a spring walk around the garden
to avoid question time in parliament
where they whitewash the story
to keep it palatable

i throw some crumbs
for the skittish mob of sparrows
a curious magpie struts at my feet
will my rambling of words be ever heard
the magpie warbles its reply
pansies turn their sweet faces
and nod

A Song for the Tree

dare I speak of trees
or dare I not speak of them
how well they clean our air
– Anon

a song for the tree

'its tiny drops of beauty fall gently through my day' – Noel Davis

as night folds away its tent
tawny owls   ringtail possums
and the bat-fly-ins
all retreat

from my third-floor balcony
the morning light
explodes with eucalypt blossoms

bee-winged branches
hum their joy
blink of stars still in the dew
and every sickle-moon leaf
applauds the dawn

as the day comes alive
the tree is a spring-full apartment block
'no vacancy' on every floor

cockatoos   yellow crests alert
swing by
as if they can't read
a ruffled crow stalks
and in a weathered hollow
balls of skin and feather
catch the sun's beam

i sit in my blue dressing gown
amid twitter and magpie warbles
in this shift of light

a dash of skink ends
in the taut neck of a kookaburra

rainbow lorikeets perch alert
on separate branches

one wings down
hovers on the bustling hollow
the exuberant tenants
feed in a squawk of orange

haiku

spring morning
the empty hollow
comes alive

the nest

with the reverence of scientists
we all lean in and wonder
at the workmanship
of this beak and claw built home

a web of reeds and twigs curl and curve
a soft twirl of lint and fleece and leaves
in tawny beige and fawn and buff
lifted by a wind   left under a tree
now here at our workshop
as a group of poets marvel
and ponder what to write

world of wings

Writers Retreat at Varuna in the Blue Mountains, 2018

a currawong flies down
to check the apples today

knocks one off   pecks awhile
declares it not ready

the gardener says the cockies are smarter –
know when the apples are ripe
without flying in to check
as if they have the date in their diary
ready for the swoop of first pick

it is an amazing garden to sit in
it is amazing to have the time to take it in

galahs sweep past
corellas fly casually by
sun speckles gold
from their spreading wings
provokes a flutter in me

a pair of red and blue rosellas
exude a charm that captivates
as they shuffle about under the oaks
and mountain pines

magpies forage for that tasty worm
sip water at the tap-dripping bowl
nod their heads   warble their song

high in the trees a butcher-bird sings
and chuckle of kookaburras
wing-clip my breath

while in the distance – grind
of bulldozer   rant of chainsaw
and snarl of traffic roar their threat
through the pristine mountain air

lamentation

'The tree breathes honey and moonlight' – Judith Wright

something was different
when i got out of the car
there was congestion in the air
a wheeze and silent choking –
still and tight
the sky was vacant
the whoosh of leaf-chatter silent

a young man
just off his pushbike
helmet in his hand exclaims –
How do they justify this?
i look down the path –
The canopies of our trees   gone.

i race to the nearest tree
extend my hand
it stands   head chainsawed
arms mutilated
a silent witness
its trunk still warm   its pulse still beats
but all twelve trees are destroyed
they stand rigid   raw
like ones who've had their tongues cut out
an apocalyptic scene
they have no voice
who will speak for the trees

in answer to my council query
nutritional stress due to lack of maintenance
was the reason given.

Thank you for your prompt reply, I wrote
I did not know the trees were sick.
I walk that path twice a week.
Those trees welcomed me
shaded and fanned me in the long months
of summer heat.
They were a godsend for walkers
well before you and I were born
so it is with great despair I write.
Who will be next?

in waiting for the jacaranda

when your time comes
there are no boundaries
your glory takes over as if
hell-bent with revolutionary
zeal to change the moment
and change it you do
flamboyantly

every year there seems a hesitation
we all speculate
about your woody branches
and the invisibility of buds
we stand in waiting
your hidden buds   shy   coy   pensive

meanwhile the children love
your Shiva-like branches
generous for climbing
where they can perch high up
and pretend they are birds

and we all marvel
when your buds emerge
and burgeon into flower

and my grandson
sweeps your purple flowers high
declaring his birthday time is here

morning glory

dawn plays into the arms
of eucalypts stretched to seek the light
and like a search for meaning
their bulbous roots
restlessly curl around sturdy rock

dew-tipped casuarinas sparkle
grass trees splurge
as if their whole purpose is to shine
self-important palms push upwards

honeybirds prowl
a lorikeet swings on a yellow banksia
magpies warble in whip-cracked air

along the creek
ferns and delicate orchids
compete with the deceptive beauty
of morning glory vines

this is an air pocket to escape the city
the creek's song has carved
into the heart of this earth for aeons

it is the human in me that delights
i know i am not needed here
and there is a loneliness in that
yet here lost from the world
i am found

old pepper tree

against my hand
crushed memory
warps time
to my childhood landscape

an old pepper tree shelters
cubby escape from adult worlds
crescendo of branches
stately curve
generous arms
for climbing and hiding
and idling in riffled breeze

wrinkled trunk
crannies for imaginary friends
and red pepper berries
to decorate handmade mud cakes

from the reach of a bough
my dad hung a swing
knotted ropes and wooden plank
for make-believe   to sit   dream
kick dust with its feel of earth
and to wing to other worlds

resilience

it seems everything this year
challenges the jacaranda

in spring its hidden buds
endure onerous drought

then whipping winds and rain
inflict a thrashing

today in the foyer of summer
in regal glory it stands

passers-by pause   as if they hear it speak
and seek to decipher its language

and there is a communal nod
for earth's generosity

a frisson of gold at the centre*

are Webb's words when he writes
about life in the gathering dark
and what I've been thinking
in this world still falling apart

things fall apart, the centre cannot hold†
yet how we wish a centring holy eye
would gleam over and over

from my balcony i watch a friar bird
nestled high in the palm fronds
lay one egg a day for four days
two to four is normal
each one is miracle enough

in the dark of night
mother bird rests on her eggs
rises to sing the dawn light
as she awaits her chicks

the gardener comes
to clear spindly fronds
i shout down
over the chainsaw
stop!   there is a nest here!
last evening i shooed away a brush turkey
didn't know they could fly this high

how long to wait?
it says twenty-eight days gestation
then the chicks to rear!
how fragile is life in a nest
in a manger
how fragile   how precious
life in a refugee boat

from the dark of a broken world
our whisper of prayer
a glint of moonlight on broken glass
a frisson of gold at the centre
light pierces the dark

* Francis Webb – 'Bells of St Peter Mancroft'
† W.B. Yeats – 'The Second Coming'

Never Can We Mourn

The greatest glory in living
lies not in never falling,
but in rising every time we fall
– Nelson Mandela

a new mea culpa

Sorry Day, 24 May 2020

if ever there was a day to grieve
so flattened by a melancholy action

that it makes you want
to close off your mind in disbelief

hold your aching heart
indeed cage your heart with steel

a day the healing song is silent
and your eyes weep red dust

when you had watched the first episode
of Operation Buffalo about the arrogance of Maralinga

and excused it as happening before we were enlightened
and the ghost of *Terra Nullius* still plagued our history books

when your mind is still etched by the ignorance
of the Taliban's destruction of ancient Bamiyan Buddhas

you realise that Australian miners have just blown up
with approval   rock shelters at Juukan Gorge

a 46,000-year cache of bones and tools
from before the last Ice Age

cutting connection with ancestors and heritage
of the Puutu Kunti Kurrama people

making Indigenous people of this country
walk in desolation   voices still unheard

and another piece of the soul of our nation
is blasted away all in the name of profit

well today is just that day

palisade

and the world is a wobbly stool
and spindly trees grow to the light
against all the odds of walls and overcrowding
and where there's a tree in your heart
a singing bird will come
and you will write of hope
with nothing to write
yet urgent to write it

The Gully*

        the creek chatters with small rocks
as it slithers along   decanted
from a swamp   succulent
as ten thousand soaking sponges
fringed with ferns   lichens   mosses
sedges   spotted with silver dew

        the rustle of a lyrebird
singing the land back to healing
mimics a birdsong world
and conceals a secret
a mountain secret

        there was a time in the Gully
when the lyrebird was silent
and the wind mimicked a deep howl
and the earth grieved and raged
for its evicted people
its ravaged concreted land

        today the lyrebird's song rolls back
a many layered history
the Gundungurra and Darug people
lead us out of a amnesic fog
with a *remember* story –
        a redemptive pathway into now

* the Gully, an Aboriginal place in Katoomba

never can we mourn

never until mankind falls
floundering
detecting the dark abyss
of human error
of ways to solve differences
of borders and walls
sects   religions   power

never till the creeping out at night
to bury guns
dismantle armour
purge the air of fear

never can we mourn
the child's death   the boy's drowning
the daughter's maiming

while operation shock and awe
defy the will
of the lone fragile world order

never while the coalition of the willing
set out with their lies as armour
the dropping of the first bombs
on that first night
televised so we watched
the city of Bagdad in the middle of the night
go up in flames
as bomb after bomb lit up the sky
bled into flames
and vacuumed the land
and we watched as we do
a fireworks spectacular
the child in us clapping jumping
more more more

never can we mourn

resignation syndrome

this poem is a repeat
written over and over
a story told again and again

the one thing different   it has a revised title
a coin
two coined words
resignation – uncomplaining endurance of sorrow and evil
syndrome – a set of concurrent symptoms.

symptoms for this poem
        vague staring into mid air
        take to bed
        not eating or drinking regularly
        not toileting
        not responding

if this is too much
imagine a child without light in their eyes

this is not a flash back
it is now
it is the Australian people
it is us the wealthy nation
wanting to have our cake and eat it too
what a cliché

using humans as a deterrent
fearful of fear
how many times do we need to tell it
how many times do we need to hear it
how many times
                until our hands and legs unshuffle
until hearts fire our country ablaze again
until we can imagine the human face
                staring out the bars as ours staring in
until we see eyes
            come alive again
until we know
it is our fear
that stifles the light

we want to know
goodness prevails over evil

humanity is a breath of us
we are it
            one breath
we breathe in each other
in depriving breath from one human
we hold it from ourselves

silence is the power
secrecy is the power
humanity   demanding to breathe together
is enough
humanity together is the power
when will we come alive to our dying?

rock-a-bye baby

soothed   cocooned…we'll keep you safe
sleep   sleep to our lullaby
rock-a-bye baby
on the tree top

tinny-eared jingle…reassures
defying zephyr-whispered warnings
and when the wind blows
the cradle will rock

short-term fixes…billions of dollars
if a child wakes   distract with distractions
for when the bough breaks
the cradle will fall

empty hands   helpless…species die
hear earth cry
and down will come baby
cradle and all

then silence… but maybe
from the silence
like green shoots from black stumps
will rise   poems of possibility.

we are sorry

there will come a time
when we bring these young ones
home from oblivion
name them
declare their age and their home of birth
admire and respect them
for their courage in their flight

if only we had the national imagination
and the heart
to do it now

for it will come to pass
a leader stands and exclaims
we *are sorry* for those who suffered
from our pacific solution
from their forced stay on Manus
for the damage done on Nauru
we *are sorry* about the temporary protection visas
for the policy of no visa
for the tough and mean treatment at our hands
in your moment of desperate plight.

and the people now scarred
by loss of homelands
and the dash of hope they held

will look up
listen
and journey on

Christchurch

fronds of the silver fern
curl

in bend of prayer
the *koru* stills
in its unfurling

autumn air falls
heavy   limp   bludgeoned out
spent
with choked cry

a park grows
flowers of love blossom
aroma of spring

in the blank space
between breaths

the pain of being human

strangers reach out
for the gentle reality
of another

air warms   fires with the haka
a country listens
it's ok to mourn

the *koru* hears the call
unfurls
anew

after the massacre

Myall Creek Memorial Weekend, 2018

when we wake to truths
that make our hearts beat fast
and walk the blood-red gravel track
that draws us down

to write the story on our heart
needle on our skin
to pin our bones into its frame
and stand

with Milton's fear
of blindness and denial

then grope and touch
the bloodstained earth
with spines of ironbark
and smell the stench of burnt flesh
where only eucalypt should waft

we weep

grapple in the dark
find that so tender songline of truth
stirs a nation's womb to birth
and know
there is no going back

all the birds

alfaia drums
moan across the land
all the birds have fled

when the mountain moves
its mud of poison tailings
waterboard down to swallow
greedily the sleeping town

only by a human arm stuck out
flag poled without a flag
the smothered are found

people dig
in sludge and rain
for loved ones   to hold again

headlines the next day
brazil dam disaster
iron ore – bonanza
shares jump   profits soar
goldman sachs   rio tinto
bhp   fortescue   and more

alfaia drums beat
moan across the land
all the birds have fled

war is over (if you want it)*

what if all the chess pieces
are white
and we play the game
with trust

what if there are no teams
no uniforms
in the twists of life –
just living

what if there is no ideology
but a patchwork of living
seamlessly stitched
piece to piece

what if there are no walls
to hem in or hem out
the view
of us

what if we all bow low
to quench our parched throats
and what if we drink
from the same waterhole

* after the exhibition of the same title by Yoko Ono

at the controls

i watch a debate
between two men
who want to crush the world
like an empty coke can
if they could get their feet
        or hands upon it

their language differs
but both
are strong about power
and rhetoric
they say building walls
        is the only way

meanwhile we float
on our tiny planet
in outer space
with a future
        so fragile

and a young child
picks up the can
and puts it in
        the recycle bin

naked before the gods

when the gods bring you a fearsome creation
the stance of a minotaur in all its horror
accept it
as if a gift you chose

study its grotesque stature
its knife-sharp teeth and eyes
as red as blood stare it down
face to face

steal from its stony wall
spare no amount of time
taming it
burn incense   sprinkle water

even holy water and goji berries
all the way from India
to match
its steely arrogance

treat it as if
brought speechless
and naked before the gods

and you –
tied to the string of some prayer
at its final heave   baring
its soft belly
knowing nothing is enough to sate its hunger
use your dagger with all your might

law of hubris

'Life is lived forward but understood backwards' – Soren Kierkegaard

his sandalled feet take space
a barricade in mocking authority
scorn pressed lips   his gaze angles down

if size could speak he shouts
his toga sweeps in arrogant folds
his arm once held in haughty pose

is lost   his eyes   once painted
to reign down terror   now blank
the lead-coloured mask of power

bleached   corrosion has taken his nose
this dictator in Italian marble
still speaks to us in syllables of stone

mudras

'In your light I learn to love,
In your beauty to make poems' – Rumi

how to make sense of it –
the hand that strikes
with such power   wrath
to take the living breath
that is life

how to make sense of it –
the hand whose touch
can heal with tenderness
to give the living breath
that is life

mudras of hands –
open   a bowl to receive
closed   weapon to reject

how to make sense of it –
of the many working to unite
of the many working to divide

a landscape called humanity

guided by divers and ropes
via a birth canal in kilometres of water
from the womb of the cave in a dark mountain
through the tightness of crevasses
hold your breath   to clamber the choke point
surrender fear   inner light
heave in the labour from death to life
why is it disasters create heroes

under monsoon darkening skies
one cannot rely on the mercy of rain gods
it is tanks of air
and an international team
navy seal divers   engineers   scientists
technical expertise
medicos and teams of supporters
that garner our attention

surrounded by a world of tragedies and suffering
it is the challenge   the pull-together
that we marvel at
holds our focus   holds our breath
its peaks and troughs
with all hope mustered
its sheer beauty
this landscape of humanity

Enigma

Is not impermanence
the very fragrance of our days?
– Rilke

delphic visitor

clear winter morning
a silver heron tiptoes
through a tangle
of wild kikuyu grass
stalks
waits statue-still
pounces
strike of pickaxe blade
throws
its rippling neck back
in an *alleluia* pose

i venture into the paddock
to capture a photo
my jeans trail over dew laden grass
and this silver heron
my morning oracle
with quiver of white breast
soft flutter of blue-grey wing
cranks its bamboo legs
uncurls its gold-tip feet
lifts   twists
tacks into flight
loose grey silk
against a blue sky

regret

slender bright bronze leaves confetti
the path   it could be any season
walking in a national park
the photo shows my family and me

i am thirty-five but i don't know it
i only know tiredness
keeping one step ahead
and feeling inadequate

life was full
shirts to iron   washing to do   shops
to be faced   food to cook
lunches to make and   mending

yes mending
a hundred tiny woes to mend
and   socks   and jumper elbows
and buttons to be replaced
homework supervised   peace kept

now i see myself in this photo
and wonder who that beautiful girl is
she is beautiful
i am sorry I didn't know her

leitmotiv

there's a garden in my hand
and the bees do not sting
my heart line pulses a balm
of sweet earthiness
after a shower of rain

rambles beyond my lifeline
along uncharted paths
to touch edges of nowhere
and trips my breath
into a million grains of air

the sun is everywhere
glows at the cusp
of my palm
rimmed and stippled
golden bright

a startle of buds
splits asunder
shakes out aromas
white roses   red peonies
sway to and fro
veined and quivering

tree branches shiver
leaves scatter
falling
a signature of stars
and settle into the quietus
of deep roots in my feet

ritual

through a crack in the door
i watch my mother
lean over the bed and kiss
my father's forehead

she turns the teapot three times
pours it into two teacups
through a silver strainer
slowly stirs in some sugar
a ritual they have done
so often for sixty-five years

now she sips her own
strokes his hand
and slowly spoons the sweet tea
into his drying lips

winter

from the window she looks out on her winter garden
with its stone walls she paved
the earth she dug   life she nurtured
and the bird bath where the birds
bow over and over their thanks to her

the long cold jacaranda branches
their tracery   like veins   tangle her heart

the dormant magnolia   its buds like her   snug tight
against cold shadows   steeped in blue

beneath spare limbs   bulbs peep
from her tenderly cared beds
presage their seasonal display

perhaps it is the light   horseshoe thin
lends itself to thoughts of death   trees lean in
songbirds are quiet   an owl calls

the dark can't touch this world
as the winter sun slips easily away

enigma

it is the magpies
their flutter deep somewhere inside
bring her back

when my mother died
i didn't know she was buried
deep in my body

i shelved her in photo albums
to be files of memory
opened on call

their song that warbles
across the landscape
every soul-piercing note

restores her
makes sense of beauty lost

memory

by the time your jacaranda
was a purple carpet of blossoms
you were gone

those last days
it was as if we wept
every last falling blossom
till only bone of wood
was a black tracery
silhouetting the sky

now in its summer shade
your grandchildren play

i can only marvel
how the earth just keeps giving

for my father

near the letter box
his white magnolia
returns spring
to our house
still grieving his loss

horizon

on the edge of a winter beach
sand falling away from under our feet
black marbling veins of seaweed swirl
restlessly

the horizon
bears down   a mirage
blurred and brooding

the last of the terns pinprick the sky
buffeted on wing   have set out
to trace a memory they do not have

anemone cling to nearby rocks
their liver-red tentacles sway
in sea
the colour of wrinkly stingray skin

wind chills to the bone
diamond cut of sand
scours my face

only my hands stay warm
joined with yours
in my snug coat pocket

pondering ducks

on the morning pond
ducks trace circles
artists of the line

first walkers arrive
ducks run into the pond
acrobatic duck show

bottoms-up diving
into pink and rippled clouds
still pond dancing

cheeky moon
smiles out of the pond
ducks pay no respect

wind

summer

bushfires
dry brown seeds
hook on my jeans

autumn

multiculturalism
gossip of leaves
enjoy the diversity

winter

wide bare sky
fallowed hills
give nowhere to hide

spring

happy wanderer
flowers and birds
obey your command

our country bypassed

as you set out for Melbourne
in nineteen-seventy-nine
your road is a long one
country towns stirring the spirit
awakening the mind
Mittagong, Marulan, Wodonga, Gundagai
Glenrowan, Wangaratta, Benalla
aromas of pubs   parks and bakeries
monuments of explorers   local heroes
and one of a dog
sitting loyally on a tucker box
re-enactments of bushrangers
and the hanging of poor Ned

your road is a long one
with pub counter lunches
Chinese cafes, paragon milk bars
ice creams and fruit stalls,
op shops for old books and 'antiques'
a fruit-fly stop   and car inspection
on the border by the Murray
with its paddle steamer on the go
brown-painted Colonial Inns
bill boards promising colour TV
which is more a flicker with the aerial just so
and luxury 'breakfast in bed' –
passed through a secret door
with the local 'rag'
by a man in shorts and long socks

and then a repeat of the day before
visiting museums and galleries
war memorials and a climb on a cannon
a walk over an historic bridge –
your road is a long one

not like today on the dual lane freeway
our country bypassed
with grey concrete and bitumen
blur of vegetation
in a confining corridor
a blinkers-on journey
blind to all the signs beckoning
but the large M meaning
a Highway Service Centre ahead
a one stop for all needs

Black Summer

We had the experience but we missed the meaning.
— T.S. Eliot

armageddon

the sheep bellow in pain
hot dry air   fires

the pointed hand on the gauge
down the highway
shouts catastrophic

the earth alight   smoky fuel
where cattle pats have dried compacted
over the past neglected century

the dams   all of them gone dry
emblazoned   cracked clay
tessellates across the land

thirst is a vampire
sucks the last drop
wracked sheep fall
there is no shade
the last trees felled in 2006

a welcome burst of cloud
morphs to disaster
the flood tsunamis
a clash of clay and torrential rain
makes glue
kangaroos bog
cattle struggle
stock stranded
stuck   they starve
stink of air stifles breath

responders
need masks   scarfed faces
like terrorists in a desert scene
an apocalyptic war zone
mosquito-borne disease flagged

but rotting smell of flesh
lures the feral
black crows shadow carrion
foxes and cats snarl in to feed
gorge carcasses
cane toads   predators in disaster
wild pigs wallow in the sticky mud
and bellow with glee

boxing day, 2019

the cicadas ring earlier
native birds call earlier too
then become silent

the summer ritual of each day –
carrying buckets of water
to top up the bird baths
is quickly appreciated

there seems an orderly queue
no boisterous bickering today
as if there is bird protocol

we all need to preserve our energy
for these days are solemn
so much loss   so much to mourn
so many birds
so many mammals
insects and living worlds lost

the smoke-laden air
can hardly be breathed
the ashened sun masked
our summer of people fleeing
livelihoods burn
metal buckles
people rescued from the beaches
refugees in their own country

we fear
        we dread
                we are in pain
for ourselves and our traumatised earth
even the south pole
ash-blanketed   melts in tears

our carefree boxing day
of cricket   tennis   yacht races
is carefree no more

i continue my summer ritual
of topping up the bird baths early
the birds fly in
splash about as if no one is watching
then sipping at the edge
keep nodding
thank you   thank you
as if they know i am watching

code red

New Year's Day 2020

when the sun like a cyclops rages fiery red
divots the sky in a coven of camouflage
it has no voice to plead 'enough'
it warns us to listen…

in the myth Odysseus gathers forces
and rams its glaring eye
but be warned
this sun is not the enemy
it is air thick with ash that chokes 'help'
amidst ember attacks and dust storms

when fish like shimmering naiads surface slimy green
float dead in display of disaster
they have no voice to gulp 'stop'
they rely on us to think…

in the myth Naiads shine silver
in springs and streams and brooks
be warned
dead fish are not the enemy
it is our river's way of weeping 'save me'
overused and desecrated

when the earth our mother is parched
her body dried and cracked
she has no voice to lament 'code red'
she depends on us to act…

in the myth our mother earth
cries for care   for respect
but be warned
cracked earth is not the enemy
it is her strangled cry 'no more to give'
exhausted and depleted

when the sea like clotted blood chokes with plastics
angry Thor thunders   floods the land
with no voice to say 'greed does not pay'
it depends on us to know...

yet still in our great city people walk about
heads down in an eerie silence
eyes weep from the smoke
behind fake masks that filter reality

and like frogs
in the myth
they are being slowly boiled alive.

inferno

the kiln burst in the flames
pots spewed out onto the ground

        when the owners returned
they stepped   hesitantly
                as if on holy ground

picked up cracked pots
                amidst charred remains
as one would loved ones   rescued

brushed off ash with tender touch
blew away dust
as if blowing life
        into memories found
beyond memories lost

bearing witness

reverence is called for

a mournful dignity on this beach today
it is far from the war zone
but each wave carries pungent remains
flanked with blackened ash

it lies to rest in curves on the sand
not stark stiff birds as sometimes wash up
blown in by severity of storms

here is death consummated
washed in
as flotsam
left like wreaths
curved around a cenotaph
wave after wave

sometimes with the change of tide
there is a short respite
for one does not know what to do
but our burnt world comes back
on the tide with vengeance

there is no escape from being the witness
one must fall down on the sand weeping

and find they're not alone
as the roll of the waves
comfort with their whispered threnodies

and hazed in smoke
the weeping eye of the sun waits

cry for a river

it's winter in a hot summer
as though the earth is in a darkened room
in her sickbed covered up to her chin
in a shroud of grey
abandoned as a withered wreath
at a cenotaph

all the rope-swinging
and water-splashing
stilled
buzz of boating and fishing
muted

how could this be us?
friendly nods become looks of dismay
state against state
the blamed and the blaming
living in denial

on the tipped over edge
the Murray-Darling our mother
poisoned with algae
chocked with upturned bodies of fish

in some parts bone dry
dying towns need bottled water trucked in
harbours of water stored upstream
enquiry after enquiry
then an investigation to assess the enquiries
as we cry
        for a river dying

When you can only take photos from the window

This virus writes its own rules.
We just have to learn them
and adjust to them.
– Dr Norman Swan

autumn equinox

March 2020

squelch of wet sand   low tide
call of seagull and tern

at the mouth of the lake
three pelicans ride
the incoming tide
each dipping its beak
in cosmic rhythm
as if trawling for last night's stars

the day warms and brighterns
i stand there in the autumn noon
sharing the sun   shadowless
balance this day between two hemispheres
and with the waterbirds
drink in its last summery light

there is no time for pause
when winter gnaws at the edge
when worrying thoughts nibble
like tiny fish
and you hear the craving
for banned picnics
in the gull's voice

i stored this moment
every sunburst and balmy smell of it
for the darkly coming
of winter days

pandemic

the birds don't know there's a pandemic
somehow they haven't got the message
they are singing more joyfully than before
or so it seems

maybe the air is clearer
the world quieter
and i hear them
maybe i have slowed down
am tuned in more
to the pandemonium of their chatter

a currawong sits high on a far ironbark
conversing with its mate on my nearby blue gum
you could say models of social distancing

but not lorikeets in the nearby grevillea
with its cascade of sweet red flowers
(more than I have ever noticed)
there dangling acrobats
look like colourful clowns at play
boisterous children preparing for a holiday
their flamboyance of vitality caught
in the morning sun

sulphur crested cockatoos fly over
a platoon with purpose
in white hazmat suits yellow-trimmed
they megaphone instructions
squawking on the wing

magpies splash in the bird bath
but don't warble   they didn't sing
all summer in our smoke-choked air
perhaps more sensitive
to the world's plight

i'm pleased they are back
their pied yin-yang gear
speaks of the harmony i seek
in this unpredictable time
where grief sits silently
on the edge

sea of uncertainty

i throw down the glass
its half empty   half full
smile of certainty
crashes

a thousand shattered pieces
glint from the floor
stark reflection of trembling tears

i weep for the glass
its loss to this fractured world
with its plimsoll line of certainty
and the choice it gave
in a sea of uncertainty

i imagine my plumb line swaying
reading the mood
weathering the storm

now each chaotic day
i still myself
wait for the ballast to settle

note to self

laughter of friends on zoom
is no more than a virtual reflection
of its cosy real life aura

top priorities –
when this isolation is over
warm greetings   warm hugs
be with family
be with friends

stay closer than 1.5 metres
inhale often the vibrance of youth
milky scent of a grandchild

crowd in as many concerts
art galleries   picnics in parks
walks by the sea

do not start the day
without first listening
for a message from the birds

note to self –
never take your freedoms for granted
ever again

when you can only take photos from the window

'I had forgotten how much light there is in the world
till you gave it back to me' – Ursula Le Guin

you can be caught easily by a showy redhead grevillea
the fancy filigree sprays of white fiddlewood florets
the yellow curl of aspen's hint of autumn

you can be caught by the one native miner
that flies in   cute and curious
and snap it from every angle with each flit of wing

yet in the window frame of my mind
it is greenery that speaks to us today
with its constancy of presence

how its algorithm of leaf space
pattern and deft design
underscores artistry

how it covers the ground
when left untamed   patient when trimmed
how it begins again   never gives up

a green tortoise of the fable
its slow slog   up trellis   over pipes
down walls

resolute against drought   fire   plague
how it regenerates   never resiles
to come back

and how the most insignificant

of weeds with lush optimism
breaks through black plastic
distorts concrete and pavement

to find the crack
the crack to get back
the light that beckons   'carry on'

it reminds me
how first green shoots of snow bells
spear apart frosty soil

how moist worlds
congregate in alcoves of rock
in the hottest of deserts

and how the play of light
shadows   slants   shines
giving us its thousand shades of green

thanks

after W.S. Merwin

in the face of our barely concealed indignation
the doctor pontificates
at this time   at your age   cruising is not recommended
now we say thank you

when our travel agent confirms the cruise is cancelled
we say thank you
New Zealand closes its borders
Tahiti fades from view
no chance to check Cook's Venusian calculations
with each port of call closing   we say thank you

for being here
to put our passports back in the safe   thank you
for our unused American visas   we say thank you
we might lament their cost
but we are grateful we didn't use them

we say thanks faster and faster
as we hear cruises called 'petri dishes at sea'
passengers and crew stranded   sick   imprisoned

for missing this nightmare   thank you   thank you
for the magic of a cruise to define the year
turned into a tragedy sidestepped
we say thank you

for the view from our window
here in our place of shelter
we say thank you
the moon   sun   merging seasons
that reassure us this isolation will pass
we say thank you

for the care of front line workers
and for the love we hold
in self-isolation
every hour of the day
we say thank you

in lockdown

today when my orbit of the world had stopped
i discovered an orbit of underworld in full swing
today when i could do nothing
i saved mosquito larvae

it began by sitting quietly
admiring spindling florets of flowers
realising the movement was not the breeze
but tiny bees diligently at work –
and getting closer
i disturbed a blue monarch butterfly

then a frog
from the disused fountain
went into song
the frog family that had left
because of the drought

i looked into the pond-shelf of the fountain
saw tadpoles   their little tails wagging nippily
a barometer of health

only then did i notice a suite of wrigglers
their world alive and vibrant
a party in full orbit   a celebration of being alive

no social distancing here
like little spinning tops they wriggled down
and wriggled up
darted around
positively drenched in enthusiasm

ah no! future mosquitos
what a nuisance they will become
but how to separate tadpoles and wrigglers
some could even be future dragonflies with red wings!

so i relented –
they all stay in their happy orbit
later i will burn two citronella candles
to clear a space where we can sit
and be safe

today when i could do nothing
i did this

the fiddlewood tree in autumn 2020

i rarely notice the fiddlewood tree that shades
the end of the terrace
a lush glossy-leaved evergreen
its hard vibrating timber
made ancient lyres and today guitars

racemes of delicate white flowers
burgeon along the branches
we smell their sweet fragrance
before we notice their shy sprays

the thing that makes me happiest today –
the bees are in bee heaven around the flowers
        and that in a pandemic
                is nature at her best.

womb-mother

'The universe is our home, our womb-mother' – Pierre de Chardin

autumn leaves
tumble
       and i   ankle-deep
in their red   tawny   amber-yellow
curled and crunchy aura
espy a patchwork of faces
mellowed with age
patinated with story
smelling
their sweet   sour   cidery aroma

i gaze down
       deep into the roots of my heart
see a grand diversity of humanity
with its majesty of oneness

i am
       liquidambar
sky-clad
my branches bared   beckoning
vulnerable   hopeful
            bearing witness
with big dreams
of newness
       surging my veins

the ocean in my heart

        tingle-brisk air jolts me
as one waking from a long sleep
the sun is high   clouds are few
i look out from Crackneck Headland
at the immensity of sea and sky
amazed at the gem-toned colours
of this world –
like forgotten smile
of a long-lost friend

        emerging from pandemic lockdown
i am astonished   refreshed
breathtakingly so
like one drinking deep
of what is undrinkable

connecting first hand
reminds me
that when i carry the ocean
in my heart
i carry a vast vision
of boundless possibility
and lightness of being
like driftwood caressing waves

being one with its beating heart
its currents
in my veins   surge   swell
i am its roar of fury
with its vitality   vigour
hard against the muscular rock
of impasse

i am its deep sighs
as its laps onto the sea shore
a sleeper whose breath rhythms unconsciously

i am the beach   mirrored
pellucid   amidst clouds in wet sand
in all moods
from tidal hours and spell of moon
to the cosmic cycle of star seasons

        despite darkness and gloom of days
i speak the language of the sea
as waves gather
curve their backs
and crash   sweep into rock crevices
        and wash away doubts and fears
        dissolving grief like salt in the sea

reciprocity

an old planet
learning from our mistakes
begins again

Walking quiet ways

> I took a walk in the woods and
> came out taller than the trees
> – Henry Thoreau

in search of the superb fairy wren

the lyrebird scratching
at the forest floor
and singing
every song she could mimic
pulls me up

i fail to see her
rustling along
at the edge of the creek
which was singing its own song
a rainy flow and fall song
delicious to hear after
the lament of summer silence

it is one of those places
with haze of blue gum air
that McCubbin could have painted
of a child lost amidst the threat
of muscular rocks
but here softened   harmonised
by moss and maidenhair fronds
shadowed by tall tree ferns
still in their stillness
eerie and lonely

i disturb a brush turkey
who trips across my rough track
like a jazz dancer across a stage

stop to touch the pink dimpled trunk
of a river gum
look up into its grandeur

then i hear them!
from the undergrowth
on the far side of the creek
the trill twittering of small birds

i still…
become one with the trees
watch their tantalising play
and salutation to the world
as they whirr with needle brilliance
along branches   their blue-brown
blur of wings   flirt   flute   fan
as tiny tails tease

once again the birds
teach me enchantment
with alert restlessness
they are there
then they are gone

so many times
i worry about our tiny birds
their bushy protective habitats
lost by urban creep
and further
by fire hazard reduction
a case of survival of the fittest

for me it was gift
to know they are not gone
just in retreat
and i am reminded
of Mary Oliver's words –
walk slowly   bow often

walking quiet ways

the walk begins on the beach
low tide and the red legs of the seagulls
look like lollypops in cloud
a cormorant dives over and over
no chance of predicting where it'd surface
coffee from the barrister
at the Lake House is worth the anticipation
(no milk at the apartment so we were hanging out)

pelicans line up for leftovers
two fisherman gut their catch
corellas preen each other
some in the trees give notes of song
while an ibis mimics elegance on a branch
where barn swallows look like notes
on musical staves   out on the lake
black swans   silky ballerinas
flaunt with their reflection

along the foreshore masked lapwings
squawk to claim their territory
and the council has fenced off
a sand area to protect
the nests of the little tern
migrated from the north for the summer

the sandstone rocks glint
with their striations and swivels of colour
showing us more than any history
or geology textbook could

as we bridge a small creek
our signature spoonbill
is again there
a caravan of ducks
feeds as it disturbs the mudflat

being in the midst of feathered angels
we return home light-hearted
our pockets filled
with the smell of sea and sunshine

dawn walk

from the jetty
snug by the blue of the Wattagan hills
softened with the swirl of mist
the lake spreads its delicate silken cloth
puffs pink with ripples
to the pattern of jumping fish

amidst a zigzag of dawn breeze
a single pelican
sweeps its beak   siphons for fish
a Narcissus fallen in love with itself
and rightly so
this land-cumbersome bird
at home on the lake
could play in a dance of swans
a reflection in symphonic balance

the sky turns from mauve and pink
to aquamarine   a waning moon lingers
a bounce of sun arrives behind me
glistens on white wings of three ibis
feeding from the muddy bank
a delicate grey heron stands tall in reeds
cranks up its body
flies off

the lake plays the shadow of birds
flying out for the day
wrinkling light fires
into brazen colour

an empty boat drifts
a lake escapee
from its overnight mooring

a cormorant with snake-like neck
dives deep returns constantly
until it reaches the jetty
clambers up
then hangs its wings to dry

seagulls pelicans and a singing mudlark
make the jetty their pondering place
i ponder too with notebook in hand
as three bossy plovers noisily declare
the jetty as their own
out further
pelicans cluster
in their hundreds on the sand island

the spell is broken
as the sun rises over the trees
and shatters the mirror of lake
into a million shards of glass
i edge back into reality
walkers pass by talking to themselves
only at close range
do i notice the bluetooth earphones

A Glad Tomorrow

To our children's children
The glad tomorrow
– Oodgeroo Noonuccal from *A Song of Hope*

garden of the gods

high on a bridge overlooking
a saltwater river
is a safe place to be
as every floating log below
could be a *hungry salty*
pretending to snooze
our grandsons scan each log
watch for signs

they spot sharklike sawfish
their wriggling serrated tails
sparkle the water with slithers of silver
young eyes find camouflaged
in the jungle sludge of the river bank
a laze of large mudskippers

we are crossing a threshold into a garden
where leaves are red pink yellow blue
stencilled with patterns of tattooed designs
and flowers ferns and palms
have evolved magical colour
adapted from Gondwana history
fill us with amazement

we meander along boardwalks
deep into a tropical rainforest
dodge dangling roots of ficus trees
dark beneath their canopy
into acres of wilderness girdled
by tangling vines and wild fruits

listen! we are on the alert
a nose knocking noise beats
a bass drum amidst flurry of birdsong
watch out! this is the wild cassowary call
the boys recognise its habitat
berries and nuts its food source
sneak along quietly

a brush turkey goes about its task
scraping back the ground
for an incubating mound
orange-footed scrub hens
skittle off our track

we stop every few steps
marvel   ponder   point
look up into foxtail palms
down into mangroves
across the paperbark swamp

the boys run wildly ahead
double back
wide-eyed soothsayers
advancing the next step of the journey

we walk through their curious eyes
as they bring our attention
      with sharp-edged delight
to focus on the myriad of small lives
insects   spiders   butterflies and bees
here is attention to our world

we have stepped into a frame
that unfolds surprise after surprise
      where we are the gods
           and this is our garden

face time by the moon

we love you to the moon and back
we confide to the brimming moon
        as it navigates the luminous sky

the strawberry moon winks with a dulcet smile
continues its journey west
        arching via the milky way

and five hundred million tiny bells
ring out their starry song
        along runnels of light

we wonder drifting into sleep
in a night that is very quiet
        where it will carry our song

an eager girl and her ardent brother
on the other side of our turning world
        sit by a window as the brimming moon

bathes them in light and they listen and see
the strawberry moon wink with a dulcet smile
        and they respond to their Grandma and Pa

on the other side of their turning world
we love you too
a thousand times to the moon and back

little mother

she sits on the play rug
with the poise of a gymnast
spreads out the shapes
in a line

her brother
sits straight-backed
cushion seat behind him
to break his wobbly falls
his bright eyes follow adoringly

triangle   square   star   hexagon
a big word for a little boy   she says
imitating her mother

a grandma watches on
and cocoons this butterfly moment
to memory

sore knees

the carpet is well worn
still it is *functional* to rear a child
who turns his bottle upside down
to curiously watch the single drops of milk drip
who throws his Vegemite toast to see what happens
and other things to which a toddler is prone

today it is just right to sit down and watch
while we play 'trains'
he has his own plan   no circuit
the picture on the box irrelevant
as the tracks are set out winding along
by the settee and under the coffee table

finally as his tiny hands fumble
the tracks click together
then the model train with its tiny magnets on each end
come into play this way that way
as he quickly learns magnetic behaviour
and has them all connected

playing my part i make choo choo noises
and push the train
as i crawl
balance on hands and knees
wobbling to the end of his track

again grandma   he says
again i crawl   shepherd the train along
he laughs   *again* he says

you play now…let grandma have a rest
i sit back
watch his little mind working
as he adds lego for a station and hot wheel cars to join in
makes them crash and brings the rescue truck

i sit back
rubbing sore knees
in a paradox of boredom and wonder
the mundane and the miraculous
grateful   to be present in this moment

L Plates

for grandparents

we should've put a sign up for the neighbours
new grandparents   enjoy the show

down the driveway
onto our street
baby on my hip
grizzling for a soothing walk
Millie the dog impatient to get going

after a struggle and two minds at work
we find the clips to unfold the pram
but then it won't move
wheels just keep jumping

Pa turns the pram upside down
and tries to adjust the wheels
baby crying   dog jumping
short with each other   we give up
carry the crying baby inside
pram returned to the garage
find another tactic to wile away the time

our daughter returns
and with suppressed laughter
looks and says
you had the handle going the wrong way
shows us more clips
for next time

it's the grandparents that are learners
prams have minds of their own
seat belts   buckles are so tight and secure
one needs to ask the child for help
food processors   sterilisers   so many parts
disposable nappies that have to be just so
portable cots that need a PhD
to set up or put away
i am told –
Milo has too much sugar
Vegemite has too much salt
i remind my kids they were reared on them
and they have turned out ok
yet they know about everything
they don't need advice
they get it all from google

the world through children's eyes

for the grandchildren

when the tide recedes towards the deep
the underbelly of the sea is exposed
for little adventurers   the rock platform
is a necklace of pools shimmering
like emeralds each full of treasure

a slip or a fall is beyond their concern
as they pivot rock to rock
clamber down on their tummies
their shining eyes
reflected in the mirrored sky
everything is magical and extraordinary

come here, quick Grandma
the crabs are humongous
a scuttle of creatures disappear in our shadow
make us wait quietly
pretend we're not there
as the rocks soften and curl
with crustaceans creeping out
their pincers like boxing gloves
point up at us.

our curious explorers learn to marvel
with respect for this living world
as they follow molluscs patterns
amidst the runnels over the rocks
as red anemones sway with waves
as they count shells
as starfish wash up as gift
as little fish and a sting ray glide past their toes

when we dig in the sand
allowing gentle laps of waves
to fill our tunnels and moats
built to protect the castles

when hand in hand we steal out
to the edge of the ocean
looking into the far distance for whales

we are in a world of wonder
and it makes me happy to be alive
and to see the world through youthful eyes

Notes

p. 35 'veranda people' – comes from the book of the same title by Jonathon Bennett. For many of us Australians live on the edge of our island continent as both stage and shelter, a retreat from hostile bushland and seductive barrier to participation in the inner world.

p. 73 'a new mea culpa' – this poem speaks out in response to the destruction of the sacred sites in the Juukan Gorge in Western Australia which occurred on Sunday 24 May 2020. Ironically the celebration of Sorry Day in Australia.

p. 76 'The Gully' – an amphitheatre called the Gully is part of the headwaters of the Katoomba Falls Creek and is therefore part of the Warragamba catchment area that provides Sydney's water. It is an ecologically and culturally sensitive place. Before white settlement, the traditional owners of the Gully – the Gundungurra and Darug peoples – used the Gully as a summer camp. Settlement at the foot of the mountains forced many Gundungurra and Darug people to resettle permanently in the Gully well before 1950. In 1957, their relatively peaceful co-existence was shattered. The traditional owners were forcibly removed from the Gully to make way for a racetrack organised by a group of local businessmen who were supported by the then Blue Mountains City Council. The trauma caused to the Indigenous community and to the land was profound – and still reverberates. The Gully was declared an Aboriginal Place on 18 May 2002.

p. 79 'resignation syndrome' – this refers to the trauma-related withdrawal syndrome, which many young refugees are suffering from as a result of the long time they are incarcerated.

p. 83 'Christchurch' – written in response to the grief and shock felt universally after the massacre in the Christchurch (NZ) mosque while people were at prayer – 15 March 2019.

p. 84 'after the massacre' – this poem refers to the Myall Creek Massacre 1836 and honours the wars fought for country all over Indigenous Australia.

p. 85 'all the birds' – the poem refers to the dam disaster on 25 January 2019 when a tailings dam at the Córrego do Feijão iron ore mine, suffered a catastrophic failure, smothering 270 people in the township below. The dam is owned by the same company that was involved in the 2015 Mariana dam disaster. Nothing had changed. This demonstrates the disconnect in our global village as one's tragedy gives another profit.

p. 89 'law of hubris' – after a visit to the Roman Exhibition in Canberra on loan from the British Museum, February 2019.

p. 91 'a landscape called humanity' – to honour the human spirit. Written at the time of the rescue of thirteen young Thai basketball players who were trapped deep in a cave on 23 June 2018 and were rescued after seventeen days while the world waited and watched.

p. 111 'Armageddon' – in the spring of 2018, severe drought exacerbated overused soil and was followed by torrential rain – disater for our land.

p. 113 'boxing day, 2019' – 2019–2020: Australia's worst ever fire season.

p. 115 'code red' – this poem was inspired one morning in the city of Sydney, the air was thick with smoke, people were in masks and the sun looked like an ominous red one-eyed cyclops hanging in a dark sky and our politicians and many were still arguing if climate change was real.

p. 118 'bearing witness' – the layers of ash and black debris washed up on our once pristine beaches was ash from a billion flora and fauna lost in the fires of the Australian summer. Black Summer 2019–2020.

p. 123 'autumn equinox' – a last walk before the Covid-19 lockdown. Hence the urgency to savour and store light for the metaphorical winter ahead. This is not just any autumn. This is autumn 2020 in the pandemic lockdown when the whole world stopped, held its breath and waited in fear.

p. 136 'the ocean in my heart' – this poem was inspired by our first visit to the ocean when lockdown was eased and I tried to write of the, then, overwhelm at being by the ocean once again.

www.ingramcontent.com/pod-product-compliance
Lightning Source LLC
Chambersburg PA
CBHW070903080526
44589CB00013B/1168